I'm Not Dying Here

Albirtha Randel

DEDICATION

To my life and ministry partner, my husband, Elton: we are fighting this war together so that we might live. When times get hard we just put our backs to the wall and start swinging with the only weapon we have.... the Word of God..

To my children and grandchildren, I love you and will fight and pray for you always.

Foreword

Family, it is so easy to sit, sulk, & stay right where you are and not fight or forge forward by faith into the potential, possibilities and probabilities that awaits you! In this book, you will glean content and gain the courage and confidence to stand and shift from your now into your next! You will discover and develop practical tools and biblical principles to help move you from your dread to your destiny! Within this book, you will reclaim the voice of a victor and not the volition of a victim! Refusing to stay stuck and stifled by fear, rather seizing and soaring by faith! As the four lepers reckoned in 2 Kings Chapter 7, if dying is the uncontrolled inevitable, they'll at least control where they'll die and how they'll die! They said to one another, why sit HERE until we die. They contemplated in verse 4, if we enter the city, the famine is there, and we shall die there: and if we sit still here, we die here. They continued and concluded, if they go into the city and fall into the hands of the Syrians, they may save them alive and they will live; and if they kill us, we will only die! And to their surprise, spoiler alert, as they demonstrated their faith over their fears, God orchestrated favor on top of favor! And as it is with the beloved author of this book, she too has demonstrated faith over fears, strength over strain and stamina over statistics and praise over problems. I'm confident, at the conclusion of this book, you too will say, I shall live and not die and declare the goodness of the Lord in the land of the living, I'M NOT DYING HERE!

Pastor A. L. Sneed II
South Austin Community Church

CONTENTS

Preface

Midway through the writing of this book, I was having lunch with a close friend and over lunch we shared our life experiences. We continued to share the struggles of life and ministry and how the enemy will attack you on every side. We shared the most recent attacks not just on us but more importantly on our families. (Don't be fooled, when the enemy cannot destroy you that mean ole rascal will use your family as collateral damage in an effort to destroy you).

I could hear the hurt in the words my friend spoke and I could feel the pain of the most recent attack. Fighting back the tears swelling behind the hurt my friend says, "no matter what I have made up in my mind that I am not dying here". I looked in my friend's face and I saw the answer that I had been searching for through months of prayer. I had been praying and asking God should I really write this book and just like that out of nowhere was my answer. My tears flowed as I shared with my friend that was the answer (and confirmation) to my prayer.

I explained to her that is the title of a book that I

had long begun to write but had not finished. Ironically earlier that week I had shared a passage from my manuscript titled "Piñata Praise" (I will share with you at the end of this preface) in an effort to encourage my friend through a difficult day. As we sat there at the table in awe of the glory of God and His mysterious ways my friend says you must finish your book to help others.

I write this book for everyone that has been hurt and thought they were dying inside but just at the brink of defeat you made up in your mind that you could not give up and you said to yourself "I am not dying here".

Piñata Praise

A piñata is beat on repeatedly. Repetitive swings are taken by either one or several individuals to break open the content of the piñata. The individuals that are taking swings delight themselves at trying to break open the piñata. We only see the piñata taking each blow as it struggles to protect its outer shell and the contents inside. No one can see (or knows) what the piñata holds inside. The piñata does not crack easily despite being vulnerable to repetitive attacks.

In order to break open the piñata one would have to hit it with enough force either once or multiple times that would cause its shell to break. Once the outer shell is cracked the piñata begins to give way exposing its contents. It is only when the shell is broken that the bounty of its treasure can be shared.

You are a piñata..... You are fearfully and wonderfully made!! You can take the blows inflicted upon you. You may be bruised and sometimes even feel broken but your outer shell is protecting what you have inside of you. When it is time God will allow your shell to be broken to expose the glory of

His presence that is inside you. His spirit and anointing will be shared with everyone that watched you take those blows!!!

The remnants of your broken pieces will tell the story of who you are despite the brokenness of your shell. Praise Him for the bumps, the blows and the bruises because your brokenness just revealed what no one else could see. God knew what was inside of you....

Introduction

2Kings 7:3-20 Now there were four men with leprosy[a] at the entrance of the city gate. They said to each other, "Why stay here until we die? 4 If we say, 'We'll go into the city'— the famine is there, and we will die. And if we stay here, we will die. So let's go over to the camp of the Arameans and surrender. If they spare us, we live; if they kill us, then we die."5 At dusk they got up and went to the camp of the Arameans. When they reached the edge of the camp, no one was there, 6 for the Lord had caused the Arameans to hear the sound of chariots and horses and a great army, so that they said to one another, "Look, the king of Israel has hired the Hittite and Egyptian kings to attack us!" 7 So they got up and fled in the dusk and abandoned their tents and their horses and donkeys. They left the camp as it was and ran for their lives.8 The men who had leprosy reached the edge of the camp, entered one of the tents and ate and drank. Then they took silver, gold and clothes, and went off and hid them. They returned and entered another tent and took some things from it and hid them also.9 Then they said to each other, "What we're doing is not right. This is a day of good news and we are keeping it to ourselves. If we wait until daylight, punishment will overtake us. Let's go at once and report this to the royal palace."10 So they went and called out to the city gatekeepers and told them, "We went into the Aramean camp and no one was there—not a sound of anyone—only tethered horses and

*donkeys, and the tents left just as they were." 11 The
gatekeepers shouted the news, and it was reported within the
palace.*

*12 The king got up in the night and said to his officers, "I
will tell you what the Arameans have done to us. They know
we are starving; so they have left the camp to hide in the
countryside, thinking, 'They will surely come out, and then we
will take them alive and get into the city.'"13 One of his
officers answered, "Have some men take five of the horses that
are left in the city. Their plight will be like that of all the
Israelites left here—yes, they will only be like all these
Israelites who are doomed. So let us send them to find out
what happened."*

*14 So they selected two chariots with their horses, and the
king sent them after the Aramean army. He commanded the
drivers, "Go and find out what has happened." 15 They
followed them as far as the Jordan, and they found the whole
road strewn with the clothing and equipment the Arameans
had thrown away in their headlong flight. So the messengers
returned and reported to the king. 16 Then the people went
out and plundered the camp of the Arameans. So a seah of the
finest flour sold for a shekel, and two seahs of barley sold for a
shekel, as the Lord had said.17 Now the king had put the
officer on whose arm he leaned in charge of the gate, and the
people trampled him in the gateway, and he died, just as the
man of God had foretold when the king came down to his*

house. 18 It happened as the man of God had said to the king: "About this time tomorrow, a seah of the finest flour will sell for a shekel and two seahs of barley for a shekel at the gate of Samaria." 19 The officer had said to the man of God, "Look, even if the Lord should open the floodgates of the heavens, could this happen?" The man of God had replied, "You will see it with your own eyes, but you will not eat any of it!" 20 And that is exactly what happened to him, for the people trampled him in the gateway, and he died.

People will cast you out based on what they see on the outside, not knowing the greatness that resides on the inside of you. They see your condition but not your character. Your character is still under construction. If people could only see that your condition is just temporary. God has a blessing waiting on you despite your condition. God will use your heartache, disappointment and discouragement to push you to your destiny. Your condition is designed to build you up not destroy you.

We find these lepers cast out of the city because of their condition. The city was experiencing a famine; people were starving physically and spiritually. The people had begun to place their hopes and faith in the king instead of God. Much like today when so many of us are struggling with our faith and experiencing financial and family issues our churches remain empty as we are seeking answers from the world instead of God. Historically when people experienced hard times and personal struggles they would turn to Jesus and the church. Today our pews are becoming sparser as people search for answers to life's problems not in the Word of God but through alternate sources. Even those of us that say we are believers struggle with our commitment to follow God. We shun away from others because of our condition and we distance ourselves from each other just as the lepers did in this text.

As a society we are dying in our isolation and separation. When we isolate ourselves we leave ourselves vulnerable to depression and open ourselves up to despair which leads to desperation. In the text we see four lepers desperate to end their isolation.

The disease was not as bad as the separation from people. Many of us could deal with our condition in private however when our problems become public the shame of it causes us to isolate ourselves from others in an attempt to hide our darkest secrets and our weaknesses. Many of us are hiding not from our problems but from the emotional by-products of our problems such as rejection, humiliation, depression, and sadness. We have allowed ourselves to become lepers. We have allowed the enemy to trick us into thinking we should just give up because everything we try, everything we touch becomes damaged or destroyed. We begin to think of ourselves as failures.

Leviticus 13:46 "As long as they have the disease they remain unclean. They must live alone; they must live outside the camp".

Some of us allow other people to tell us we are unclean and unworthy and should be set apart from others. No one has the power to deem you unworthy when Christ has found you worthy and has already redeemed you. Do not allow anything or anyone separate you from Christ. When we isolate ourselves in seclusion we allow the enemy to creep into our thoughts. We lose focus on Jesus and shift our concentration to our problems. We grieve the spirit of God when we allow negativity to dominate our thoughts and action.

If the enemy can inhabit your thoughts then he

can control you. Our thoughts hold the key to our destiny by controlling our actions. The enemy will manipulate your situation and have you thinking opposite of the plan and purpose God has predestined for you. You can stay in seclusion or move to a place of elevation.

Your pain is just a diversion designed to derail you as you travel to your destination. Do not allow the enemy to divert you from your destiny. Do not allow the enemy to put up smoke screens that prevent you from seeing the promises of God. You have a purpose but you have to endure some uncomfortable situations in order to receive your promise.

Had it not been for the leprous lesions the four lepers would have never discovered the treasure that God had laid up for them. Somewhere between their shame and seclusion the lepers realized that they were surely dying at the gate. So they made up in their minds they could either die in their situation or risk it all at a chance to live. In their current position death was certain. What are you willing to risk for a chance at a better life?

The lepers were facing a perilous plight. Two things were weighing heavily on them. There was a famine in the land and they had been identified as lepers, therefore sent out of the city. Sometimes God will dry up and separate you from your resources to get you to move towards Him. He will move you from despair to desperation. Elijah was enjoying life at the brook until the brook dried up. He was forced to move from his place of comfort to a place of restoration except Elijah could not see the promise of restoration. God will sometimes camouflage our blessings in the pain of our burdens.

You may find yourself in a dismal dilemma hanging between the decision of giving up or pressing on. You can either stay where you are or you can get up or move; the choice is yours. You can wade in your shame, waddle in your misery or you can get up and move. Even the prodigal son made the choice that enough was enough. He would rather be a servant at his father's house than to rut around in the hog pen. It does not matter if it is the gate of the city, the brook or the hog pen. When will you say enough is enough?

The lepers were afraid because they knew that outside the city they would be unprotected and vulnerable. However, they did not know this was part of God's plan for them. He has to put us in uncomfortable situations in order for us to seek Him for protection. When we feel protected we also feel a sense of security and our fears will begin to fade. The lepers were no longer afraid of the unknown but rather looked forward to what might be. When we face our fears and insecurities then we can also face our demons. Then and only then will we find out that Jesus has already slain our demons and has been waiting for us to claim the spoils of victory. When we face our fears we will realize that God has already removed the very thing we feared and then we will come to know and understand the protection and promises of God.

You might have some things in your life that look like they may never heal. You might be isolated and separated from people in your life. You might be in a famine searching for any scraps of love, joy or peace. In your desolation do not be distracted....stay focused on Jesus. Build your faith. Study the Word but most importantly tell yourself, "I'm not dying here".

CHAPTER ONE
WOUNDED WORSHIPPER

Even when you decide to get up and fight you must know that you will take some hits; no battle is without battle scars. With any battle there will be setbacks and the wounded……………..

Wounded Worshipper

Luke 8:43-48 43 and a woman was there who had been subject to bleeding for twelve years, [a] but no one could heal her. 44 She came up behind him and touched the edge of his cloak, and immediately her bleeding stopped.

Whether you know it or not, every week during worship service we encounter the wounded worshipper. Anyone can be wounded and worship, it does not matter which church you attend or your denominational preference. The wounded worshipper is there trying to conceal their wounds. They may sit unobtrusively in the back hoping not to be noticed or they may be the one inordinately participating in worship attempting to disguise their hurt. They can be the usher on the door, a choir member, an elder, or even your pastor. They may have been hurt by the church, loved ones, or simply beat up on by life. Nevertheless, despite their wounds, they worship alongside of us every week and we are unaware of their personal struggles. Perhaps that wounded worshipper is you?

Visible Wounds

Sometimes we are bleeding and are unaware of the source of the bleeding. If it were not for the visible evidence of blood we would not seek help. The woman with the issue of blood was bleeding but had no idea the source of her affliction. The one thing she knew was that she needed help. She sought out help in all forms until she was exhausted physically, mentally and financially. Many of us find ourselves in similar situations. We seek help from sources that offer little or no assistance but serve only to drain us.

Physically we look for people to heal our wounds. We give ourselves to them only to be left with a deeper wound. We look for acceptance that might heal our wounds of self-esteem. We vie for the attention of others even if it cost us our own self-respect. We hide our hurt behind clothes, shoes, or other material things that have little or no value. Jesus shed His blood for us because He found value in us. We have to understand our self-value to slow or stop the bleeding. We become emotionally wounded as we allow others to devalue us. Our hopes and dreams that once motivated us now only torment us. We become battered and bruised as one thing (or person) after another continually lets us down and we find our drive to thrive slipping away from us. Mentally we accept the situations we are in and accept that there is no escape. We lose hope. Without hope we see our situation as impossible.

When I find myself in difficult positions and lacking strength I remember the scripture my mother taught me in my youth, *"...what is impossible with man is possible with God". (Luke18:27).*

Perhaps my mother knew I would need these words to get through life and she was preparing me or perhaps she used the same scriptures for her own source of strength in the face of her own adversity and pain. In either case she knew that not by our strength but only by the strength of God that we would be able to overcome the trials, tragedy, disappointments and heartbreak that were intended to mortally wound us. We ourselves cannot get out of our situations but with the help of God we can achieve the impossible. The woman with the issue of blood had tried to heal herself and used her own means to heal her problem. It was not until she made up her mind to try Jesus that she would find true healing. We must come to realize that Jesus and Jesus alone is our one and only true source of complete healing.

Financially and emotionally we invest in people and things without a return on our investment. As we make these investments we relinquish a part of ourselves in hopes of reciprocated or mutually acknowledge feelings. We wait patiently for any sign of validation that the other person is just as in love as we are but to no avail. We attempt to validate the relationship by investing in expensive gifts as we wait patiently on any sign of validation or reciprocation. Be careful not to invest too much of yourself into people or things that will leave you void and empty handed. You will make yourself vulnerable and susceptible to manipulation and even greater pain.

As we connect with one another and develop interpersonal relationships we must be mindful to maintain a healthy balance.

Without a healthy balance we will be left with deep wounds and scars that may lead to emotional detachment. You will put up walls and barriers in an attempt to keep from being hurt again. These types of wounds may be difficult to heal as you struggle to recover from the devastating and possibly embarrassing experience.

Invisible Wounds

The lack of evidence of an injury does not suggest that a person is not hurting. Sometimes the source of our wounds cannot be identified.

Loneliness, rejection, isolation and emotional trauma

are wounds that can leave us wounded and emotionally hemorrhaging.

Our emotions can affect us both physically and spiritually. Our pain can manifest itself into physical symptoms such as decreased sleep, lack of energy, fatigue or noticeable changes in personality. These types of wound do not fade away but over time they will grow and manifest into more serious issues. Perhaps if these wounds were visible we could offer assistance to each other. We would either seek help ourselves or allow others to help us. We would be mindful not to cause or add additional stress or stressors. We would be less judgmental and more compassionate.

Unfortunately these wounds are not visible. These wounds hide under the cloak of denial. They mask themselves beneath superficial smiles or overly enthusiastic personalities. The pain they hide can only be revealed when all the walls that contain their secrets are torn down. It seems easy but years of self-protection have built an almost impenetrable wall of defense.

Sometimes our emotional pain will cause us to hurt others. You know what they say, "hurt people, hurt people". The church is filled with individuals that are hurting but go unnoticed. Failing to recognize those that are hurting only perpetuates and prolongs the healing process. The primary source of most church hurt occurs due to an unidentifiable wound. However if we dive deeper we will find that perception may be the root cause of the underlying issues or perhaps the secondary source of the wound. Perception is how one views a particular situation. One may perceive that actions or conversations are directed towards them due to unresolved issues or wounds of their past. Likewise personal unresolved rejection or humiliation experiences outside the church may spill over into the church. Similar to our personal relationships, church hurt can also occur when an individual experiences a lack of validation when their financial, emotional or physical investment goes unreciprocated. Usually these are due to unrealistic expectations that individual places on the church.

How do you recover from hurt within the church? How do you heal from the wounds of gossip or malicious conversation or rumors? First pray for those that persecute you. Jesus was mocked and beaten for sins He never committed. How did He get over it? He prayed for those that persecuted Him but mostly He loved them. We must follow Jesus example and we most love those that speak ill against us or those that try to hurt us with their words or actions.

John 13: 34 "A new command I give you: Love one another. As I have loved you, so you must love one another. 35 By this everyone will know that you are my disciples, if you love one another."

Self-Inflicted Wounds

Our wounds may be self-inflicted due to the hurt from our past. We allow the memories to replay over and over therefore we never allow ourselves to heal from the pain. Our lives become mine fields as the people around us walk gingerly and cautiously around us to avoid setting off an explosion. Bitterness becomes the norm and we lash out or blame everyone else. Nothing is ever our fault because to make such an admission would mean we would also have to acknowledge the pain that is buried deep within us. The wounds spread throughout our lives causing us to hurt those around us. We end up pushing the people closest to us the farthest away from us.

It is not until we accept and/or acknowledge who or what has caused the pain that the healing process will begin. Weeds grow right alongside good grass. You must pull the weeds from the root to totally remove the weeds otherwise the weeds will just keep coming back and spreading. You will only reap good fruit when you plant in good soil. We cannot expect to reap a good harvest when we sow seed of deception and discord.

Often times it may be the ones closest to us that

are able to inflict the greatest pain. Many of us are dealing with the pain of betrayal which in some cases can be as painful as physical wounds. Once a trust has been broken it is extremely difficulty to trust again.

Psalm 41:9. Even my close friend,
someone I trusted,
one who shared my bread,
has turned[b] against me.

It is only those closest to us that are able to hurt us the deepest. Do not let the dissolution of the trust and friendship causes you to become angry and bitter. These types of wounds will only fester and spread to other areas of your life. Instead we must follow the example of Jesus when Judas betrayed Him (Matthew 26).

We cannot overcome the pain of betrayal in and of ourselves; we need the help of the Lord. Do not take matters into your own hands, turn it over to God.

1 Peter 3 Do not repay evil with evil or insult with insult. On the contrary, repay evil with blessing, because to this you were called so that you may inherit a blessing. 10 For, "Whoever would love life and see good days must keep their tongue from evil and their lips from deceitful speech 11 They must turn from evil and do good; they must seek peace and pursue it. 12 For t e eyes of the Lord are on the righteous and his ears are attentive to their prayer, but the face of the Lord is against those who do evil.

The key to healing is forgiveness. We must allow ourselves to not only forgive others but we must forgive ourselves. By allowing yourself to forgive you are also freeing yourself to begin to heal. It will not be an easy task to forgive those who have betrayed you or hurt you. It will take an inner strength that is manifested in your prayers by the Holy Spirit. The bible tells us to pray for our enemies and those that persecute us (Matthew 5:44). How can I pray for my enemies when I cannot even stand to think about them or even say their name? All we want to do is forget not forgive. But do we really forget or is it just buried deep within us only to surface when something happens resembling the initial hurt. Or perhaps someone reminds you of the person that offended you? In either case the memories rise to the surface as quickly as an erupting volcano and become just as volatile. When we fail to forgive we give that person or thing power over our lives and we are kept in bondage by our past. When we do not forgive we harbor negative feelings of bitterness and hate.

Pray for the strength to forgive and then pray for peace. Forgiveness will free you of the burdens that hold your emotions hostage. Once you are released a wave of peace will come over you and you will finally be free of your past. Replace the bitterness and hate with love.

Take the focus off your pain and those that have hurt you and focus on Jesus. He can heal you if you just let Him.

You may be wounded but you will not die. You may be feeling weak now but in God you can be made stronger.

CHAPTER TWO
DYING OF THIRST

John 4:13-15 13 Jesus answered, "Everyone who drinks this water will be thirsty again, 14 but whoever drinks the water I give them will never thirst. Indeed, the water I give them will become in them a spring of water welling up to eternal life." 15 The woman said to him, "Sir, give me this water so that I won't get thirsty and have to keep coming here to draw water."

Thirst is a craving to drink. It is typically associated with dehydration which occurs as a result of lack of fluids. The brain will signal a craving when there is a lack of water. Many of us are dying of spiritual and emotional thirst and we do not even know it. We have been totally depleted by heartache, disappointment and a lack of love leaving a very deep void in our lives. We have taken so many hits and suffered so many losses in life that it has left us dehydrated emotionally and spiritually.

We have so many people pulling on us from every direction. In ministry we have donned so many hats and taken on so many tasks that it leaves us mentally and physically burned out. We have given so much to others until we are left empty and completely depleted.

The expectations we have placed on ourselves as

well as the expectations of others have literally drained and depleted our reserves and sometimes our resources.

Request and demands from others flow like rushing waters and we find ourselves drowning in the currents and in need of rescue from the very ones that demand our help but to no avail we find no one. Our desire to please one another and our lack of ability to say no have left us running on empty physically, emotionally, financially, and most important spiritually. To fill the void we find ourselves chasing and craving anything to fill the emptiness.

Water is a metaphor for life and thirst a metaphor for a desire for everlasting life. Water is essential to all life. Without water we will surely die.

While serving in the military, they would tell us to always make sure we carry our canteens and to ensure our canteens were filled with water to avoid dehydration. I disliked water and would fill my canteen with all types of drink other than water. As we stood in formation the platoon sergeant would come around checking the contents of our canteens. I was prepared. I had two canteens one that I would have for the inspection and one that was the canteen I filled with my sugary drinks. I found myself thirsty all the time. Little did I know that those drinks would only give me a temporary satisfaction to my thirst but would soon wear off leaving me even thirstier? Many of us are filling the voids in our lives with things that give us a quick, temporary satisfaction. Only the living water offered by Jesus, can truly quench our thirst. Once we accept the water He offers we will not thirst for the things of this world anymore.

We spend too much time chasing our creature comforts that only offer us temporary gratification but when we chase after Jesus He offers something that will last forever.

The woman at the well was dying of thirst. As the Millinennials would say this woman was thirsty. Millennials use the term thirsty to suggest someone is overly eager or desperate. She was emotionally empty inside. In her desperation she latched on to whomever and whatever could fill that void she was experiencing in her life. Her lack of satisfaction and discontent with her life left her emotionally and spiritually bankrupt to the point she had lost value in herself. Perhaps she had unfulfilled goals or dreams. Disappointment now replaces the hope she once held dear to her heart.

Her self-esteem and self-worth completely severed her attachment to others as noted by her visiting the well at a time when no one else would be at the well. Then she encountered Jesus at the well. Jesus recognized her emptiness as well as her eagerness as she attempted to fill her emotional void with men. The woman went to the well alone to escape the judgment of others. She was a Samaritan, a group of Jewish people that married and mixed with the Gentiles, which were frowned upon during that time. She was an outcast. She went to the well at the noon hour to avoid the crowd. Some of us come to church with the same mentality of the woman at the well; we come in late or leave early to avoid people.

Mostly she was WOUNDED

She was emotionally empty and felt unworthy.....

She lived in the shadow of her past as it weighed her down and she could not move forward. She was wounded by her past and never healed from it. That is why she had relationship after relationship as she lived in the shadows of her past which kept her enslaved. Like the Samaritan woman many of us carry the baggage of past relationships with us into subsequent relationships. We remain in relationships that are unhealthy and self-destructing. One of the main reasons we stay in these relationships is usually out of comfort or convenience.

Jesus and the disciples were on their way to Galilee. They did not have to go through Samaria but Jesus knew that He was on a mission. Sometimes it seems that the path we are on is out of our way....that we could take an easier route but that is not the plan God has for us. He takes us the long way around on purpose. Had Jesus taking the easier route He would not have encountered the woman at the well. He knew His purpose.

He knew there was a WOUNDED WORSHIPPER AT THE WELL DYING FOR A DRINK.

How many of us are wounded and because of our wounds we find ourselves dying for drink? How many of us are thirsty and need some water?

Although Jesus was tired and weary from His journey He put aside His own needs to attend to the needs of the woman. Despite her history, Jesus still accepted her. Jesus did not judge her He only ministered to her with truth and love.

We try to minister to folks with the truth (keeping it real) but there's no love in it and that's why we hurt more than we help. If we want to be real about it we must allow ourselves to be transparent. We must be willing to tell the dirty truth of our past so that others might be saved by our testimony.

He told her the truth about herself but in a way she could hear what He had to say.

She was humbled by her encounter at the well.

You can't encounter Jesus without first confronting the truth of who you are and then the reality that you have to change. A transformation occurs when you meet Jesus.

The Samaritan woman leaves her water pot at the well after her encounter with Jesus. We have to learn to leave our problems at the well. Leave our burdens at the well. Leave our pain at the well. Leave our old life behind at the well and run tell everybody about the man you met at the well.

What we leave behind will be replaced with far greater things. Stop holding on to who you think you are and reach for who God wants you to become.

It is difficult to find happiness with others when we are unhappy with ourselves. Search for what truly makes you happy and not the things that fulfill everyone else's happiness. Superficial satisfaction is fleeting and once the high of it wears off you are left with an even deeper state of dissatisfaction. Become your own best friend. When you learn to spend time with yourself you will be better company to others.

Self-validation is the first step to learning to love you. Self-validation is accepting your own experiences, your thoughts, and your feelings. Stop judging yourself with such a critical perspective. Others will never accept or believe in you if you do

not accept and believe in yourself. Accept your
failures and your losses based on your own set of
standards not those set by others. Be honest with
yourself about who you are and embrace the real
you. Learn to comfort yourself with phrases of
affirmation. Replace the negativity in your life
(people, places or even your job) with encouraging
and motivational positivity.

Focus on your personal strengths. Learn to love
yourself and laugh often. Others will be attracted to
your joy.

CHAPTER THREE
DYING TO BE SEEN

Luke 19:1-10 1 Jesus entered Jericho and was passing through. 2 A man was there by the name of Zacchaeus; he was a chief tax collector and was wealthy. 3 He wanted to see who Jesus was, but because he was short he could not see over the crowd. 4 So he ran ahead and climbed a sycamore-fig tree to see him....

Many of us have found ourselves like Zacchaeus, wanting to not only see Jesus but for Jesus to see us. We try to acquire status and wealth in an attempt to be noticed. We are in a constant struggle for position in our homes, our workplace, and even in our church. We attempt anything and everything just to be noticed. In our desperation, we fail to see that it is not our position or our status that allows God to see us but rather our character. He is not moved by our finances or how well we can sing, pray, dance, or preach; He wants to know how much faith we have and how big is our heart.

Zacchaeus was the chief tax collector of Jericho. He held a position considered high in statue unlike his physical appearance. He was a short man. Perhaps that is why he treated the taxpayers so miserably. He carried with him an unrealistic sense of superiority, due to his stature in society. However because of his physical stature he also carried a sense of inferiority which emotionally and psychologically crippled him. He believed himself to be better than everyone else. He was not happy with himself so he set out to make everyone else miserable. You know people like that, don't you?

He had what many would call short man syndrome. He was a little man physically but pretending to be big to cover for his shortcomings. Many of us have the short man syndrome too. We think of ourselves as bigger than what we really are sometimes. Because he was short he wanted people to fear him and reverence him hoping this would make up for what he lacked in his physical appearance.

Romans 12:3 For I say to every man that is among you, through the grace given unto me, not to think of himself more highly than he ought to think, but to think soberly according as God hath dealt to every man the measure of faith.

When we exercise our faith in humility God will see us as giants amongst His people. True power is meekness under control. When we learn to control our own selfish desires and operate in love then we will be able to understand what it means to have power and position. Zacchaeus used his power and wealth to make others miserable. Why is it that when we are lacking in an area we try to cover our shortcomings by over-exaggerating ourselves in other areas.   We find ourselves being just like Zacchaeus at times.

Zacchaeus had a handicap that was emotionally and psychologically disguising him from others but not from God. Are our handicaps, the things we are deficient in, keeping us bound in a web of deceit and deception?   Instead of overcoming our handicaps we use them as excuses.   Excuses keep us from reaching our potential and promise that God has for us. Excuses are nothing more than shadows of our fear that looms over our lives, crippling us so that we are unable to move forward.

As Jesus passed by Zacchaeus found himself unable to see over the crowd.   Here he was the chief tax collector yet no one was willing to help him.   Be careful of how you treat people.   You never know when you might need their help.   Can't you see him jumping and struggling just to get a sneak peek? We are unable to see what God has for us due to how we have treated others. He is withholding our blessings until we stop trying to be seen by others and we seek to be seen by Him.

Zacchaeus was in a high position but because of the veil of lies that clouded his mind, he was not small enough to see Jesus. Has Jesus ever passed you in your high place but you were not small enough to see him? We boast about our jobs. We brag about how we climbed the ladder of success when we should have been trying to climb the sycamore tree to see Jesus. We stick out our chest and do not give a second thought about how God blessed us to get there. We give credit to our hard work and sacrifices but not to God who gave us the strength to not quit. We have problems with the "I" syndrome. I made it, I this, and I that. It is not only a character problem but a vision problem. Our "eye" has stopped seeing God. We only see ourselves and not in our true form but we see ourselves how we want others to see us. We set out to make a reputation for ourselves and we don't care if it is good or bad.

Your reputation is driven by you character. Reputation is synonymous with character and the two are easily confused. Your reputation is what other people think about you and your character is an individual, distinctive trait that refers to your morals and values.

Your reputation is what people say about you but your character is what you say about yourself. You can't control what people say about you but you can, through your character, control what you say about yourself.

In this text, Jesus' reputation was that of notoriety and good character. He had been traveling the country side healing the sick and teaching the good news while little old Zacchaeus was being treacherous.... Robbing and stealing from the poor old taxpayers of Jericho. In contrast they both had a rep, one good and the other not so good. They both got their reputation by way of their character. You are not born with your character. Character is developed over time. Character is a set of qualities or values that shape our thoughts, actions, and feelings. It is the combination of traits, either good or bad that form your nature. Good character means that you have strong morals and values. But your character can be corrupted by bad company. An old Japanese proverb says, "When the character of a man is not clear to you, look at his friends". Your external factors can affect your internal character. You are who you hang around. Big Momma used to say it like this, "if you lie down with dogs you get up with fleas" or you might know this one "birds of a feather flock together". When I was younger I used to think my friends could not make me or break me! I told myself I can hang out with my friends that smoke weed: that did not mean I had to smoke weed just because they did it. Yet over time I found myself wanting to be like them. The bible says *"as a man thinketh in his heart so is he" (Proverbs 23:7KJV)*

Jesus had a Godly character. His heart and mind was on God's law and he became a doer of God's word. Zacchaeus was curious about this man called Jesus. He was curious about this man's reputation and his character. So much so that he had a strong desire to see Jesus. Jesus' reputation had preceded

Him and this made Zacchaeus curios (and desperate) to see Jesus. He had heard about him, heard of Jesus reputation and found himself wanting to know more of this man called Jesus. How many of us have a reputation that leave people wanting to know more about us?

Zacchaeus had heard Jesus was coming so he ran ahead and made plans to climb the sycamore tree to get a better view of Jesus. This tells us we have to prepare ourselves to come into the presence of Jesus. We can't let our problems hold us back from the goodness and the glory of Jesus. Zacchaeus wanted to see for himself this man they called Jesus. Zacchaeus knew he had a shortcoming but he was determined not to let this hinder him. His desire to see Jesus was stronger than this small obstacle.

How many of us desire to see Jesus for ourselves regardless of the obstacles that stand in our way? Zacchaeus decides to climb a sycamore tree to overcome his shortcomings. What are you willing to do to seek Jesus? He knew he had to elevate himself to just get a glimpse of Jesus. To be with our God in heaven, we can't stay at the level we are at right now.

If you have been going to church for a while and no one can see a change in you then you might want to find a sycamore tree to climb so you can see Jesus. We can't stay in the position we are in if we are going to see the glory of God. We gotta change our position. If we are too high we gotta come down. If we are too low we gotta rise up. Otherwise, we will never be able to see Jesus or He us.

The bible tells us that when we were babes in Christ we feed off milk but as we grow we should be on meat. Some are still on milk despite attending church since they were a child. The bible tells us we have to study God's word. 2 Timothy 15 says it like this, "study to show thyself approved." Study and get off the milk. It is time to grow up or at least graduate to Gerber toddler foods. Bottom line you cannot stay in the same place with all your excuses, handicaps and imperfections and expect to see God or have Him see you. Now don't get it twisted... He sees you just not the way you want Him to.....you should want Him to see you in the light not the darkness.

Jesus met Zacchaeus at the very spot that Zacchaeus was at. That is good news for us. If we just seek Him, He will meet us where we are. So if we are struggling with insecurities, fear, anxiety, self-worth and self-esteem we just need to change our position. Stop standing and start kneeling.

Jesus told Zacchaeus to come down out of that sycamore tree. How did Jesus know his name? How did Jesus even see him? Jesus saw his heart. There is no hiding our heart or heartaches from Him.

Depression, loneliness, and rejection these are all devises the enemy uses to deceive us into thinking we are nobody and invisible to those around us. You are not invisible, Jesus sees you. Jesus knows you by name just as He knows the stars in the heavens. He knows your name and He knows your heartaches. Your problems do not go unnoticed by Him. He can call you out of any problem or situation. Even when we attempt to hide from the worry of sickness, the heartbreak of death and the anguish of grief we cannot hide from the one that sees us when no one else can. He sees us and is there to comfort us. Just as we search for the things we have lost, so does Jesus search for us when we are lost in our pain and sorrow. He not only sees you but He loves you and His love is enough. He loves us enough that He does not wait for us to find Him. He searches for us even in the darkness. The path you are on now may be dark but even in your darkest moments Jesus is waiting to be your light. Wherever your life's journey leads you, Jesus will meet you where we are.....

CHAPTER FOUR
DYING TO UNMASK

Psalms 139:1-4 "O Lord, you have searched me and known me! 2. You know when I sit down and when I rise up; you discern my thoughts from afar. 3. You search out my path and my lying down and are acquainted with all my ways. 4 Even before a word is on my tongue, behold, O Lord, you know it altogether."

Who am I? How did I get here? Will the real me please step forward? Many of us have found ourselves asking ourselves these questions as we grapple over our identity.

Many of us are suffering from an identity crisis due to misguided and unrealistic expectations placed on us by either ourselves or the expectations of others. As we explore our identity we may encounter confusion and uncertainty. Our uncertainty and confusion leads us to a place of insecurity where we begin to question who we are and where we belong. As we attempt to achieve these expectations we are left with disappointments and dissatisfaction which leave us lost and searching for answers and feeling lonely or helpless. We find ourselves in a desolate place searching for answers to our identity.

The repetition of these scars have left us hurt so many times over that the scars that remain have left us unidentifiable even unto ourselves. Thus we find it easier to hide behind the masquerade of our lives by donning a mask than to face our issues. Relational, financial, and spiritual issues often lead to our own uncertainty and confusion of who we are therefore we often walk around in masquerade. We don masks to cover our true self- identity from others and often even ourselves.

We are living in duplicity, hiding the truth of who we are from others to avoid their judgment. We don masks in hopes to disguise the pain and scars of what lies beneath the surface. A battered woman will attempt to hide the bruises of abuse not to protect her abuser but to cover the shame of her own weaknesses. She becomes skilled in covering her wounds and her secret. Usually, these women have low self-esteem that they hide behind a mask of false strength. Low self- esteem is usually the primary reason a woman will stay in an abusive relationship. Something on the inside has deceived them into believing they are not pretty or worthy enough therefore they stay in the relationship. The Word of God tells us that it is through our weaknesses that He is made strong. We must identify our weaknesses, addiction, pornography, adultery, stealing, gambling, cheating, and even telling those "little white" lies. No matter how big or small we all have issues that we battle daily. We cannot fight these on our own without Jesus. Jesus tells us to cast our burdens upon Him.

Due to our human nature everyone desires to be

accepted or to belong. Therefore, we will don masks to cover the heartbreak of rejection. The hurt leaves a void in our lives that leaves us searching for approval and acceptance.

Masks allow us to hide the lack of confidence we have in ourselves. This lack of confidence is spawned from a fear of judgment. Judgment from others that is unrealistic and usually unsubstantiated. Society has erroneously taught us gender- specific ideology that has confused us and distorted the truth. Men were taught at a young age to be strong, quit acting like a girl. So men grow up and learn to hold in their hurt and pain in fear of appearing weak. They are also taught from birth to be strong and never cry otherwise they will appear weak. When in reality men who are more in touch with their emotions are much healthier spiritually and emotionally. They have better interpersonal relationships and are no less "stronger" than their counterparts.

Like men, women have also been taught conflicting ideologies that are just facades to mask the truth. Women are taught to disguise both their inner and outer strength. These are unrealistic stereotypes that aid in suppressing our confidence in ourselves and birthing low self-esteem. Those that refuse to shed these stereotypes are responsible for perpetuating these false images and playing on the beliefs and fear of others.

2 Timothy 1:7 For God has not given us a spirit of fear and timidity, but of power, love, and self-discipline.

Through the power of love we can overcome our fears and remove our masks. Only God has determined who we are and our true identity is revealed through Him.

Masks allow us to camouflage our fears and insecurities with false courage and strength.
Without our masks we are left exposed and vulnerable to our weaknesses. Many of us adapt the mentality and mantra "fake it to you make" in an effort to hide our inadequacies. We are afraid to ask questions or just say "I don't know". Fearing that our lack of knowledge will make us appear inferior to our peers. The word of God admonishes our fears by reminding us we have nothing to fear. He will always be with us and will strengthen us.

Isaiah 41:10 Amplified Bible 10 Fear not [there is nothing to fear], for I am with you; do not look around you in terror and be dismayed, for I am your God. I will strengthen and harden you to difficulties, yes, I will help you; yes, I will hold you up and retain you with My [victorious] right hand of rightness and justice.

Fear is a tool the enemy will use to distract you. He will use your fears to confuse you and shift your perception. Fear will permeate your thoughts and shift your reality. Fear will stop you in tracks and stagnant your progress. Perhaps the greatest weapon against us is fear. But as believers we have to guard our hearts and our minds against the tricks and the devices of the enemy. Do not allow yourself to be distracted by what others say. Hold firm to the Word of God and stand boldly on His truths.

Pastor A. L. Sneed II once said, "Let nothing and no one distract you or disconnect you from His presence or His promise."

When we allow ourselves to become distracted or disconnected from God we allow ourselves to become vulnerable. Our weaknesses are amplified and used against us. We stop hearing from God and stop believing what God says. We seek to become what we see and hear on the television, the radio and on social media as a way of being accepted. We will put on masks to hide the truth of who we are from others (and ourselves).

Perhaps one of our greatest fears is the fear of rejection. We spend hours concentrating on our physical appearance to be accepted by others. Men will wait for hours at the barber shop waiting on that one barber that can "cut them up right" yet fail to make things right in their homes or at church. Women will sit hours having her hair braided followed by a trip to get her eyebrows waxed but will leave a church because she has been hurt. If we can endure physical pain for vanity then how much spiritual pain can we bear? The reality is we do not want to go through any pain, any trials, or tribulations due to our own self- centered selfishness. We don't want to work in the church because we have been hurt or perhaps we want to avoid being hurt not knowing that it is in our hurt and our pain that God makes us better.

Outwardly we attempt to conceal what is going on inside of us but our Father in Heaven can see beyond our facades. We do all this just to look better. WHY? Because it also makes us feel better. Yet the root of it is our vanity. The nail salons, beauty and barber shops, and gyms comprise a major portion of our weekly time schedule. We will pay gym memberships and visit the gym multiple times a week until we get the results we desire. However, we murmur and complain about going to church more than once a week, multiple services on Sunday, or if church services go beyond the time we think it should end. We must put time and effort into building up our spiritual body as much as our physical body. A big beautiful house is worthless if the inside is not maintained.

God sees through our masks and see the real US. He sees us without our makeup. He sees through all the masks and makes our lives transparent to HIM. So we then must become transparent to one another. Instead we attempt to recreate our identity but we cannot re-create what God has made. He has created us for a purpose.

Go easy on yourself. We can be our own worst critics. Many of the battles we fight we usually fight with ourselves....our biggest opponent. We will encounter hardships and disappointments along the way; these are all designed by God to shape and mold you into the person who will become. Use those experiences as bridges to the next level of your life. Do not burn these bridges as you cross over them because you may need to cross them again to help someone else cross over. Your trials are intended to train you for the battles that lie ahead. With every battle you will get closer to your victory.

The reality is we have covered the pain of emotional trauma, disappointments and rejection with so many different masks that when we see ourselves in the mirror even we appear foreign to us. We have learned to adapt by leading a double life. We become one person at work and another person at home. And when we attend church we become yet another person. We say we are believers but our actions say something totally different. Most people will call this being two-faced or having two faces. That is what we are with God....two faced. We sing His praises and shout on Sunday morning then on Sunday evening, we are cussing each other out. Two-faced. Who are you? Do we even know anymore after years of duplicity? We serve a real

God but are we being fake with ourselves and with each other.

"25 Therefore each of you must put off falsehood and speak truthfully to your neighbor, for we are all members of one body." Ephesians 4:25 New International Version (NIV)

We have to remove the masks. Transparency is our greatest asset not a weakness. We have to let each other know that we get tired, we get weary, we hurt, we cry and we have issues....... It's time to unmask. Tell those around you that I'm taking off my mask.

Will the real you please step forward?

CHAPTER FIVE
DYING TO LIVE

John 10: 17-18 17 The reason my Father loves me is that I lay down my life—only to take it up again. 18 No one takes it from me, but I lay it down of my own accord. I have authority to lay it down and authority to take it up again. This command I received from my Father."

Dying to live is an expression that suggests an eagerness or yearning to live life to its fullest potential. Every moment should be lived with enthusiasm and enjoyment and without regret. Unfortunately we have limited our lives by restricting our thoughts and actions to conform to what and how others have told us to live. Others will try to deceive you or manipulate how you perceive your life. Whose report will you believe? We cannot live our lives based on others views. Are you living your life to the fullest or are you just going through the motions?

Do not let anyone take from you what God has given you. The power lies in you through Christ whom has given each of us all the ammunition we need to not only fight but to be victorious. Every day we must fight to live. Find something to live for; find a purpose that will drive and motivate you to be better and do better each and every day. Anything worth having you are going to have to fight for it. The decision is yours.

Our biggest battles are fought in the most treacherous and difficult battlefields....the battle field of our minds. Our minds can be dubious, over shadowed by doubt and fear. Fear will cause us to hesitate which allows the enemy to get the proverbial "drop" on us. Doubt is probably the more deadly of the two because it gives birth to mistrust which will manifest into a lack of faith. Once doubt seeps into our minds the battle is lost long before it can be fought. Lack of trust will undermine the fabric of our faith, not just in God but also in God's people. We will not be able to discern the Holy Spirit when it is sent to protect us. Our lack of trust will have us putting our trust (and faith) in the wrong god and the wrong people. Money and material things will become our god.

Jesus laid down His life freely so that we could get up from our mistakes, our heart breaks and our disappointment. So get up.....you are not dying; there is more in you and more that God has for you. My Mom would always say to us, "Just keep living child". She told us we would experience different things in life and would go through many trials and tribulations. She would also constantly remind us that there is nothing under the sun that has not been done. Therefore as I think about the phrase keep living child I am reminded that we have a whole lot of living yet to do and a whole lot of experiences yet to overcome. So keep living and you shall be victorious.

You are going to make mistakes, accept them and learn from them but most importantly move on from them. You will be hurt and you will be disappointed but we must not allow ourselves to harbor unforgiveness in our hearts. When we fail to forgive those that hurt us that weight of unforgiveness becomes like a ball and chain that keeps us shackled to that individual. We must first learn to forgive ourselves before we can forgive others. Otherwise we will find ourselves prisoners to our own emotions.

Emotions can cause a chain reaction of devastation. We must be willing to go deep into the painful places to receive healing. Own your triggers, the things that set you off. Accept responsibility and work through your issues. If necessary seek counseling either by your pastor or by trained professionals. Your issues should not become a mine field for others where they cautiously try to navigate around your unpredictable emotions.

You control your thoughts and actions. The power to live free is in your control. Do not be enslaved in a prison designed for you by someone else. You hold the key that will release prosperity and purpose in your life. You just have to believe and trust that Jesus knows your condition and will call you out of it.

> *John 11:43 When He had said this, Jesus called in a loud voice, "Lazarus, come out"!*

That place you thought you would die is not your final destination. Lazarus death was only a temporary condition. Many of us are in temporary conditions that if we are just patient and wait on the Lord, He will call us out of it.

Dianna Ross has a song titled *"I'm Coming Out"*. The lyrics went something like this:

> *There's a new me coming out.......And I just had to live. I think this time around......I am gonna do it*

> *Like you never do it.........Like you never knew it*
> *Oh, I'll make it through*
> *The time has come for me........To break out of the shell*
> *I have to shout..........That I'm coming out*

> *I'm coming out.......I want the world to know*
> *Got to let it show........I'm coming out*

The song talked about letting the world know she was coming out. It implied that she was different, that whatever was holding her back would not hold her back anymore. She was brand new. She was going to be positive and let it show that whatever was in her past was back there......she was coming into her future.

I am sure that she had been through some things, had some trials that tried to take her out. She had been in a situation that she did not see how she was going to escape. She told herself that if I get out of this I'm going to have a new attitude. What attitude do you have about your situation?

How you think about your situation determines how you will overcome your situation. If you believe you can and will overcome there is almost nothing that will hold you back.

John 11:41 So they took away the stone. Then Jesus looked up and said, "Father, I thank you that you have heard me. 42 I knew that you always hear me, but I said this for the benefit of the people standing here, that they may believe that you sent me."

Lazarus had to die for God to get the glory and for the people to believe. It is difficult for us to believe when everything around us suggests that we can overcome adversity on our own without the assistance of God.

Trials build you and strengthen you so that when you come out you are better and stronger. You must be willing to dig deep within yourself to find the gem that lies inside you.

Diamonds are buried deep within the earth. They must be excavated but when excavated they cannot be distinguished from the dirt. They have to be shaken and sifted to remove the dirt and expose the diamond. In the process the diamond gets jarred around as it bumps around in the tool used to sift the dirt.

God is just shaken and sifting us to expose the diamond inside us. He has to sift us and as part of the process we might get beat up some. The best part is that after the dirt is removed everyone will be able to see the splendor of your beauty that lies beneath the dirt. You are just a diamond in the making. Be patient your heartaches, disappointments and even your failures will be removed to expose the diamond that is in you. Our blessings are buried deep within us but we must go through the excavation process.

Those things that are buried deep within us can be called forth just as Jesus called for death to let go of Lazarus. When we fail to let go of people and things that are holding us back or remain in places God told us to leave we find ourselves dying slowly. Some things that are killing us we have to give over to Jesus. He has the power to release those things from over your life.

As we read John 11:44, Lazarus came out still wrapped in his death linens. *Jesus spoke to them take off his grave clothes and let him go.* You have to die to the old you but when you come out leave that old stuff buried. Speak to your situation and tell it to let you go. Stop being burdened by stuff that will hold you back from living the life Jesus is calling you into.

Years ago my Mom was diagnosed with at least two separate heart issues that should have taken her life on two separate occasions but it did not. The enemy was determined to break Mom's spirit by devising another attack on her body, this time with a diagnosis of cancer. She never stopped giving God the glory or the praise; her spirit nor her faith ever wavered.

Through it all Mom continues to speak life and not death. Although she is prepared for death she has made up in her mind that she will live despite her diagnosis. Even the doctors are amazed that she is still doing remarkably well. Out of obligation (and curiosity) her doctors see her twice a year routinely primarily just to see if she is still alive and well because they know there is nothing more they can do. She says that she is not worried because she knows someone that will never fail and will never leave her. Therefore no matter what you are going through speak life, not death.

When I was young Mom not only taught me but she had me memorize Luke 18:27 *"what is impossible for man is possible with God"*. This has become my life's mantra. Whenever I face an impossible situation I remember how God works best in impossible situations. I know that He will work it out for me if it is His will. He will give me the strength to overcome. He will provide me the weapons that I will need to fight and He will give me the endurance to keep fighting when I want to give up. He knows the plans He has for me. I just have to trust his timing. When we pray we pray with expectation for immediate results. God may not answer our prayers in our time, it may take years. I remember listening to a well-known evangelist talk about how she prayed for her son to be delivered. She prayed and she prayed. Years had passed but she never stopped praying. After 20 years her son was delivered. The bible tells us to pray without ceasing. If your prayers are not answered yet just keep praying and never lose the faith. If your prayers are not answered don't stop praying. It is in those times that we must trust God even more. When we trust and believe in God despite our circumstances it builds our faith and character.

Your circumstances and conditions are designed to build our character. Because of Mom's condition I have learned to pray harder and seek a deeper relationship with God for myself. Sometimes your trials are not about you but are for someone else to see the glory of God through you.

CHAPTER SIX
DIE TRYING

Matthew 19:26 Jesus looked at them and said, "With man this is impossible, but with God all things are possible."

When I was young my Mom always told me to shoot for the stars. She would always encourage me to never settle for less but to push myself as far as I could go. In high school I used that phrase as a principal focus for a short essay that subsequently allowed me to win first place in the district essay contest. Since then I have added to that premise by saying as you shoot for the stars do not worry about falling short because you will be higher than you are now.

Things will not always be easy in life but we must keep pushing and pressing. God has promised us life and life more abundantly but it comes with a price.   To follow Him means we will go through some hardships, grief, discomfort, despair and prosecution. We will encounter difficult moments that will make us want to throw in the towel. When things begin to look impossible that is when we should look to God. Nothing is impossible with God. No matter what adversity you face if we hold firm to our faith and trust God we will be able to overcome anything......with God's help.

There will be moments of doubt....stay focused. Abraham and Sarah doubted and even laughed when God promised them a child. Many of us have missed our blessings because of doubt.

James 1:5-8 tells us not to doubt but simply believe. When we doubt we are easily swayed to this doctrine and that doctrine. We must believe and take God at His Word. It is easier for us to believe in each other and be let down over and over than to believe God.

Doubt will make you want to give up. Negative thoughts will begin to take root and grow, spreading like weeds into your thoughts, your heart and your spirit and eventually choking out what God has planted inside you. Replace them with positive thoughts, prayers and affirmation of faith.

People will doubt you but you must not be overshadowed by their doubts and speculations or opinions about you. Do not allow their negativity to drag you down. Find a way to rise above the naysayers and listen to the voice of God. He has already placed inside you everything you need to be victorious.

After overcoming so many odds and the shadows of their past failures the Kansas City Chiefs football team found themselves playing in Super bowl 54 for the first time in over 50 years. With only minutes left in the fourth quarter they found themselves down by a 10 point deficit. They could have easily surrendered to the disappointment and allowed themselves to be discouraged but they refused to allow their setback distract them from their goal. They refused to give up. The commentators and spectators doubted that they could win due to the amount of time left on the clock. The Chiefs however, had a different mindset. They knew as long as there was still time on the clock that victory was still a possibility. In life it is a matter of perspective, you can either say you don't have enough time or you can say there is still time on the clock. It's time to change your perspective.

We must push past the urge to quit and suppress our overwhelming desire to complain. In our lowest moments when we feel that time has expired on our hopes and dreams we must realize that as long as we are still breathing we still have time. Some of our biggest victories only come based on the depth of our desperation. Do not allow your weaknesses to become the source of your demise. When we are weak, He is strong.

"My grace is sufficient for you, for My power is made perfect in weakness.' Therefore I will boast all the more gladly about my weaknesses, so that Christ's power may rest on me." 2 Corinthians 12:9

Draw on the power of the Holy Spirit to minister to you in your time of emptiness and weakness. This is not the time to be isolated from others. Use your spiritual weapons of prayer and praise to battle the spirit of defeat. Do not allow yourself or others to make you feel defeated or deflated. You will encounter battles intended to derail you from your journey. These are merely minor setbacks. You may see them as a weakness but God sees it as an opportunity to flex His power and display His glory.

When you first begin to workout you feel weak and wimpy but the more you work out the stronger you become. Resist the urge to give up or stop exercising at the first sign of progress. You are stronger but you have much more work to do. In the same manner do not give up if you fail to see any progress. Trust the process.

When we were young the only thing many of us could think of was the moment we would grow up. I, myself, repeated numerous times how I could not wait until I was grown so I could do what I wanted. Then the time came when I became an adult and with it came big adult problems and responsibilities. No longer could I blame someone else or expect my mother to "fix" my problems. I, alone, had created these problems most of which because of my sinful nature. Not only did I desire what I was not prepared for but I also pursued things/people that were not good for me. All of these things have now become my burdens and my cross. I was living without Christ. The Word tells us, "What good does it profit a man to gain the world but lose his soul". I was lost all because I was dying to live not for God but for me. Something had to give. I could no longer live not like this. Something or someone had to be sacrificed but I had no idea that somebody would be me and that something would be those things I put before God. That me, the one I had become comfortable with and accustom to, that me had to die.....

Hezekiah was told he would die. He turned to the wall and prayed. When we are in our darkest hour this is not the time to talk to everyone. Everybody can't help you nor can they understand what you are going through. Turn from people and turn towards God. Get to know God for yourself and have a relationship with Him.

Things will look bleak and almost impossible but we serve a God that is a master of impossible situations.

Have you ever been faced with an impossible situation? Perhaps you are have struggled or you are currently struggling with a failing relationship, financial problems, difficult and unruly children or perhaps you are struggling with addiction or perversion. You are not alone if we could all be honest we have either had the same issues or we are currently fighting the same demons.

After trying everything you begin thinking nothing or no one can help. You feel as if you are carrying a sack of bricks while slowly sinking in quick sand. Every time you overcome one hurdle there are ten more in your path. You feel hope has abandoned you and find yourself overcome with despair and depression.

When you face an impossible situation, remember faith and prayer can ignite the possibilities of God's power. Hold onto your faith and put your hope in Christ Jesus. Surround yourself with people that are willing to embrace and encourage you unconditionally. Remember the bible story of the cripple man whose friends lowered him through the roof just to see Jesus. What type of friends do you have around you? What type of friend are you to others?

A man brought his possessed son to Jesus to heal him because no one else not even the disciples could heal his son. We search for others to help us when all we have to do is look to and seek Jesus for ourselves. When we finally throw up our hands in frustration and defeat that is when the door is opened for Jesus to come into our hearts.

Only when we trust and believe in Jesus Christ will we be able to truly accept the impossibilities of our Lord and Savior.

Ester is another example of trusting and believing despite being in a desperate situation. When the Jews faced execution at the hands of Haman, Ester faced a dilemma. How could she fight for her people, the Jews, without risking her own certain death?

She fasted and prayed despite her insurmountable and what appeared to be hopeless situation. She faced death but despite it all she put all her trust in God. You may have lost all hope but do not fret God will give us hope in the midst of our hopelessness; all we have to do is trust Him.

Everything is possible for one who believes (Mark 9:17-23).

Both Ester and the man with the possessed son believed God for deliverance from their situation. What are you trusting and believing God for in your life? Your situation is not too big (or too little) for God to handle. You just have to give it to Him and let Him be God.. We will have disappointments and we will become discouraged but do not focus on your problems but focus on our God. Our struggles are great but our God is greater.

CHAPTER SEVEN
DYING TO STOP THE PAIN

Ministering while bleeding

2 Corinthians 1:3-4 Blessed be the God and Father of our Lord Jesus Christ, the Father of mercies and God of all comfort, 4 who comforts us in all our affliction, so that we may be able to comfort those who are in any affliction, with the comfort with which we ourselves are comforted by God.

Wounds and feelings of brokenness are all too common in life and when you serve in ministry. The impact of ministry can manifest pain, sadness or anger that sometimes goes ignored. As you continue to work in ministry these feelings slowly and continually escalate until they rise to the surface and are projected onto others, especially those closest to you. Like a volcano these feelings appear to sit dormant but deep under the surface there is something brewing just waiting to spew its fiery contents and leave nothing but devastation in its path. The volcano mantle, the place between the core and the crust is broken allowing lava to erupt. Don't let your mantle become broken. Protect your core.

We need to take time to rest and recover from the

work (ministry). Never think you are not expendable. Although you are valuable to the ministry, rest assured in the event that something happens to you, the ministry will continue without you, especially if you do not take care of yourself. If you are emotionally, spiritually and physically unhealthy due to stress you are more of a risk to the ministry than an asset. Take time to ask yourself what is the source of your motivation and drive? Is it the Spirit of God or are you attempting to compensate for unmet personal needs? Are you ministry driven by the looming shadow of failure? Or perhaps you thrive off the attention due to unresolved self-worth or self-esteem issues? These are questions we must honestly ask ourselves as we lead and serve in ministry. As we serve God we should put away conceit and deny our own selfish needs. When working in ministry you must examine your own life, your motives, your heart and your intentions.

Philippians 2: 3-5 3 Do nothing out of selfish ambition or vain conceit. Rather, in humility value others above yourselves, 4 not looking to your own interests but each of you to the interests of the others. 5 In your relationships with one another, have the same mindset as Christ Jesus:

We put too much pressure on ourselves and take on too many tasks. In ministry be careful not to take on more than you can comfortably handle. It is ok to say no sometimes and to allow others to help you. Taking on too many tasks can leave you feeling frustrated and resentful. The things that once brought you joy are now a source of discontentment and detestment. You will begin to dread ministry or anything that is ministry- related.

The first step in overcoming your pain and hurt is acknowledgement. Be honest with yourself about your feelings. Allow yourself to feel the pain. Don't deny feeling sad or angry. Allowing yourself to feel will also allow you to focus on the pain. When we continually ignore the pain it allows that affected part to become injured repetitively which only causes even deeper pain. When we overwork our bodies physically our bodies will begin to exhibit signs of overuse through pain and swelling. These are indicators that the body needs to rest. Our psyche and our spirit will also exhibit signs of overuse letting us know that we need to rest. It is important in ministry that we balance life and ministry.

It is easy to minister to others when we are broken but sometimes we deny our own feelings and thoughts. It is during these times that we must earnestly seek God and make time to be in His presence. Allow Him to minister to you. Take a break and take time to heal. Time for rest and restoration is critical for your mental and spiritual health. It is ok to step back or step down for a while until you have recuperated and fully recovered.

Don't return too soon otherwise, you will only cause further injury to yourself or others.

Many years ago I fractured my ankle. I rushed the recovery process and did not allow my injury (or my body) to fully heal. I cheated myself when it came to physical therapy because it caused pain. I had forgotten the "no pain, no gain" mantra. I just wanted to get back to life and work. Now many years later, I continue to have unresolved issues with that ankle because I did not trust the process and follow the steps to recovery now the same or similar pains keep resurfacing.

In ministry unresolved "church hurt" will continue to cause pain because we don't allow ourselves to heal properly. We fail to trust God's process. We dive back into the very thing that caused the pain hoping things will be different. Take time to allow God to heal you and make you stronger. Don't rush the process.

How do you minister to the very ones that are the source of our pain? This is exactly what Jesus did when He sacrificed His life for us. Jesus knew Peter would deny Him, Judas would betray Him and the people would turn on Him yet He still pressed forward to His destination.

Jesus knew He would be hurt emotionally, physically and spiritually by the very ones He came to save but He chose not to give up. Jesus willingly went to the cross knowing the sacrifices and burden that He would endure. We will encounter what might seem like insurmountable deficits but we must not allow ourselves to be defeated or deflated.

Do not avoid people for people are the source of your calling. Be careful not to push people away. However you should find a trusted circle of friends that you can confide in and trust. It is in this circle that you can "let your hair down" and be transparent without judgment. Not everyone can handle your transparency or your personal struggles so chose your circle of confidants wisely. Also release your pain and problems through prayer and meditation.

The burden of ministry can be a heavy load to carry. You will be constantly bombarded with prayer requests of others that require the burden of confidentiality. This can become a heavy weight to carry daily. Therefore, ensure that your own personal prayer life is not only strong but safeguarded and fortified. Pray for your own spiritual health. Pray for strength to continue the journey and not quit. Trust God. Perhaps He is using your wounds to take you on a deeper journey with Him and desires for you to trust Him regardless of the situation. Pray to follow the teaching and life of Jesus by exhibiting compassion to those that have wounded you.

CHAPTER EIGHT
DYING TO SELF

*Matthew 16:24-26 If anyone would come after me, let him
deny himself and take up his cross and follow me."*

Traditionally we have been taught "to carry our
cross" figuratively as a symbolism of our burdens
and problems. However the cross represents so
much more. The cross represents love, forgiveness,
freedom, purpose and redemption. It is at the cross
that you obtain these things after a symbolic death to
self. When we relinquish our old thinking and let go
of people, places or things that weigh us down then
we receive a new life….in Christ.

When Jesus said take up that cross He was letting
us know that we would have to die to self and that
we would have to do this daily because this Christian
journey is not just a onetime event but it is a daily
sacrifice and daily commitment. The cross is not
just a representation of our personal burdens but
also a reflection of the burden of being a follower of
Christ. Enduring humiliation and persecution is part
of the cost of carrying the cross and following
Christ. In order to receive everlasting life we must
be willing to make sacrifices.

Many of you are probably thinking why do I need to die? The death spoken of here is a spiritual symbolism not a physical death. It is a choice to relinquish your old life and lifestyle. It is a sacrificial and transformational mind changing event. This transformation must transpire both mentally and spiritually. When we change our thinking we are able to achieve a spiritual transformation.

I am reminded of the metamorphosis of the butterfly. In its caterpillar state it will shed the protective casing around its body to emerge as a beautiful butterfly. The transformation does not occur instantly, there is a process. Some of us dread this process. The journey will either paralyze us in our fear or push us deeper in our faith. The power is in the renewal and reformation of our mind. Before we begin the process we must ask ourselves what we are willing to shed in order to become.

As a defense mechanism many of us have engineered a protective casing around our lives to protect our emotional and spiritual health. Unfortunately the protective barriers we erect as protection are also keeping us in bondage. These barriers stunt our spiritual growth and development by enslaving us in our own thoughts. It is time to break free and embark on a fresh new journey to becoming a new you.

The first step occurs in the battlefield of our mind. Let down your defenses and allow Jesus to give you the spiritual weapons you need to defeat the demons of destructive and deceptive thinking. It is impossible to be a butterfly with a caterpillar mindset.

We must be willing to shift from a self-centered life to one of serving others to be a true believer and follower of Christ. Jesus tells us to take up our cross but we often forget the later part of the verse in which He says, "Follow me". Follow me... is a call to emulate the life of Christ by abandoning our current life and/or lifestyle just as Jesus did when He came to be our Savior. In order to achieve a life with Christ we must deny our carnal thoughts and desires. We must put those thoughts and desires to death if we are to achieve everlasting life. We will be required to sacrifice who we are for who we desire to be in Christ.

Jesus knew the struggles we would encounter and He knew we would struggle with these things daily. He knew the weight of these things would seem unbearable at times. We may stumble or even fall from trying to carry such a heavy load. It is not the fall that keeps us from our destination but rather the fact that we allow ourselves to succumb to the heaviness of what we are carrying. We allow the pressure to be greater than our purpose. We take our focus off the destination and instead focus on our problems. We recite "take up the cross" as a mantra to our life struggle but we ignore the latter part of the verse "follow me". We miss it because our focus is not on Jesus but on our problems. When we allow ourselves to shift our thinking from our situation to our Savior the weight of the cross becomes insignificant.

There are times we look at others and envy the strength that they exhibit in extreme situations of despair, disappointment, dejection and dashed hopes. We wonder how they could be so strong. Or perhaps you may have manifested the same display of strength in difficult times in your life? The answer is not in the how but in whom. That Whom is Jesus Christ. The Word tells us we are made strong in our weakness.

2 Corinthians 12:9-11 But he said to me, "My grace is sufficient for you, for my power is made perfect in weakness." Therefore I will boast all the more gladly about my weaknesses, so that Christ's power may rest on me. 10 That is why, for Christ's sake, I delight in weaknesses, in insults, in hardships, in persecutions, in difficulties. For when I am weak, then I am strong.

The grace of God is greater than any problem we encounter. That is why your problems and predicaments did not destroy you. While others are watching you managing and coping with your situation they fail to see how God is working in the background. He is holding you up giving you strength to overcome the torment, tribulation or task that was intended to take you out. This is not the time to give up hope. It is in these times that we must guard our faith. We all believe in Jesus and we all have faith but there are times, if we are honest and transparent, that we are unsure or we have doubt. Something occurs in our life that puts a crack in your foundation of faith.

> I remember sitting in that courtroom and hearing the judgment of 35 years declared over my niece. Even now writing it still seems so surreal......

The one thing that stood out the most from that day is breaking my charm bracelet. The bracelet contained charms with the inscriptions of love, faith, believe, and pray. As I scooped the bracelet off the floor I noticed one of the charms was missing. There laying a short distance from the bracelet was the charm inscribed with the word "pray". That was the message God was sending me. I needed to pray and not react. In my moment of weakness God was reminding me He was still with me.

The bible tells us to pray without ceasing something we forget when we are deeply troubled. When we fail to pray we disconnect ourselves from God. This is not the time to disconnect but rather that we draw closer to God. When we fail to pray we allow the enemy to enter through these cracks in our foundation. The enemy will place destructive and malicious thoughts and behaviors in our minds in an attempt to pull us from the Father.

Do not allow yourself to crumble under the weight of the cross. Jesus never said following Him would be easy. The Word says to take up thy cross and follow me. The cross is not light nor does it come without burdens. In those moments that we feel hopeless and helpless we must reflect on Jesus and how He suffered for us and gave His life so that we might live.

That day in the courtroom left me wounded and broken. I was in disbelief. I was dismayed but mostly I was distraught. 35 years not only echoed in my mind but it ripped through my soul to the core of my faith. I had been praying. I had been serving. I had been faithful. Yet I sat there wondering God did you hear me?

In that moment I felt my foundation giving way. Any moment I felt as if I would be sucked into a sinkhole. As I was struggling to cope with my shattered faith I saw that others were looking to me as a source of strength yet I had none. Then I reflected on the charm bracelet. I was weak and I needed the strength of my Father in Heaven, if not for me at least to be strong for the family.

It is amazing that no matter how much you are hurting when you help others in the midst of your pain it provides a balm to your wound to stop the bleeding…. at least temporarily.

In the midst of my brokenness a classmate calls me to ask about faith. I was battered, bruised and bleeding and in no condition to talk about faith when I was struggling to hold on to my faith. That conversation was the balm I needed to stop the bleeding. As we spoke I began to realize that yes, I was beat up but I was not broken. The words of life and affirmation that I was speaking to my classmate were actually providing healing to my own spirit. I thought I was speaking life to help someone else but God was actually using my words to them to help me to minister to myself. I remember when I was preparing to counsel people in ministry one of my old pastors would tell me to never use my own words use the person's words and that's exactly what God did to me; He used my own words to convict me.

No matter what you are going thru, no matter the sentence they have given you; no matter what the doctor say….just seek the Lord in prayer. Pray for Him to strengthen you and give you peace to accept His will and not your will. After you pray, then you have to trust Him. Trust that He knows what is best for you.

Faith is believing and trusting God despite what you may or may not see. Faith is believing in His infinite wisdom, that He knows what we need. It might not always feel or look like we want but we still have to keep the faith. Faith is submitting to God's will. Again, His will won't always line up with our wants (sometimes it does). For this reason so many lose faith because we have been praying and believing God for what we want and when it does not come to pass we lose faith. He still hears our prayers and He desires to give us what we want but like a good parent He knows how to hold back. He holds back not out of spite but out of love because He knows that some things we are praying for is not good for us.

Jesus knew what struggles we would encounter on our Christian journey. He knew that we would suffer hardships, financial instability, emotional trauma, and relational conflicts. These are all things that Jesus took to the cross with Him. These are things we carry with us daily so He says to us pick it up and carry it.....not carry it as a banner of despair or a burden of disappointments put as a reminder that our cross, no matter how heavy or troublesome it can be overcome through our self-sacrifice.

It is a daily struggle to push past your own hurt and your own problems for the sake of others but that is why we "take up our cross" as a reminder that the cross is symbolic of what we must endure in order to become.

You might be bleeding, you might be bruised and you might be even feel broken don't fret because you still have breath therefore you still have time to change.

It may feel like you are dying that's because you are, at least the old you. You will arise from the ashes a new creature. This is just your transition. Just as you transitioned into adulthood from a child, this too is growing pains. It hurts now but the new you will be better. Your pain has a purpose. Jesus died as a sacrifice for our sins so that we might live. We must die to the flesh in order for our spiritual man to live...eternally.

To take up thy cross is symbolic of love, sacrifice and service. Jesus loved us enough to endure the pain of the cross. He sacrificed His life for ours and all He asks in return is for us to do the same. He desires for us to serve others even if it comes as a sacrifice but most importantly He desires for us to love one another. Love bears all, love endures all but let us never forget that love forgives all. Forgive yourself and move on; discover the beauty that resides deep within the fortress of your mind.

Next time you adorn your cross jewelry take a moment to reflect on the sacrifice and everything else that the cross represents. It has greater meaning than an accessory to your wardrobe. It was at the cross that our lives were forever changed.

Colossians 3 1Since, then, you have been raised with Christ, set your hearts on things above, where Christ is, seated at the right hand of God. 2 Set your minds on things above, not on earthly things. 3 For you died, and your life is now hidden with Christ in God. 4 When Christ, who is your[a] life, appears, then you also will appear with him in glory.

The entire third chapter of Colossians reminds us that we have to give up the things of the world to live for Christ. Let us remember that we are in this world but not of this world. This world is only temporary. We must set our sights on things eternal. Everything of this world will rust, be eaten by moths or fade as in a vapor but the things of God will last forever.

I'm Not Dying Here

CHAPTER NINE
DYING FOR MORE

Moving From Here to There

Matthew 26:36 Then Jesus went with his disciples to a place called Gethsemane, and he said to them, "Sit here while I go over there and pray."

Here and there both used to describe location or position. The term here focuses your attention on what is in front of you and what is in the present. Here as opposed to there. The term there is also used to describe location or position but it suggests something that is a distance away from you. We have two terms that indicates your position by representing the present and future; here and there. To get there I cannot stay here. Moving from one position to the other is about a choice. It is all about a state of mind.

We take a car, a bus, a train, a boat, and even a plane to get from one destination to another. Most of us do not care about the mode of transportation instead what matters most is simply getting to the desired destination.

The destination God has for us cannot be obtained by these means of transportation. Matter of fact I do not know about you but how I get there does not matter as much to me as me just getting there! In order to reach our destination it will require change. Change is an inevitable part of life and is necessary to move forward. However change is never easy and may at times appear very daunting because of the shadow of the unknown. Moving forward can be very mysterious and for this reason many opt to remain in their current position without discovering their passion or purpose.

Jesus knew His purpose and His destiny. Both had already been set. Many of us are still in search of our purpose. This pursuit is a common thread we all share. Usually we find our purpose in the midst of our pain and struggle.

Jesus goes to the garden of Gethsemane to pray. In the garden He prays 3 times as He struggled and wrestled with His destiny. He knew what He had to do and He also knew what He had been sent here to do, nevertheless, the flesh struggled with moving from His here to His there. Physical, spiritual and emotional transformations occur when we make major alterations in our lives. Anxiety takes a front seat in an attempt to take over the decision making process. It will try to convince us that we are better off staying where we are because what if this happens or that happens. Then fear will jump in the car as we struggle with the decision to take flight or fight. It may affect us physically with symptoms of heart palpitations, increased heart rate or sweat.

These are all distractions in an attempt to confuse us and take us off course. This is the time we must pray and pray fervently as Jesus did in the garden.

The only way to overcome major storms and barriers in our lives is through prayer. When Jesus sent out the disciples they came back saying they could not cast out the demons. Jesus told them those types of demons can only be cast out by fasting and praying

When we struggle in the flesh that battle is best fought in the spirit with prayer. Some things we go through we can only overcome by prayer and fasting especially if we are about to embark on a major change.

Jesus knew what His future held. He knew the overwhelming and arduous circumstances He was about to endure. But more importantly He knew He could not stay where He was; He had to press through it to get to His final destination.

Jesus took Peter, John and James with Him to the garden but told them to stay here while I go over there to pray. While many of us are connected to our communities and our companions, it may be necessary to leave them behind on your journey to your destination. Let go of unhealthy relationships that block you from a deeper and more meaningful connection to the cross and to Christ.

Jesus said stay here....Perhaps He knew that the type of burden He was about to endure that even those closest to Him would not or could not understand or comprehend. The text illustrates that not everyone in our circle will be able to comprehend what we are going through or will go through. Stay here.....Leave your community or companions if they are incapable or if they lack the type of faith necessary for the task at hand or for the journey. Peter, John and James had been with Jesus as He performed miracles and healed the sick. Yet they still exhibited little faith. Not everyone you know can go where you go. We all have different levels of faith.

When Abraham took his son Isaac to sacrifice him....he told the men with him, you stay here.....

The things God is about to do in your life everybody cannot be there to witness.

"You stay here I'm going over there to pray" is what Jesus told the disciples. Learn to give yourself over to private time with God. Make time to converse with Him in the still and quiet moments of your day. His voice will be a comfort to your troubled heart. As much as we desire to tell God about our problems take time to just listen for His voice.

Psalm 46:10 "Be still and know that I am God"

It is in those quiet, still moments that you can converse with God uninterrupted and without distractions. When you go alone you reduce the possibility of distractions. Some of us find it difficult to go anywhere without an entourage. Leave your entourage and isolate yourself so that you might hear from God without all the noise. When we have too many people around us they can stifle, repress or restrict us from reaching our destiny.

Even those closest to you cannot go where you go. Your destiny is just that....it is yours. To go from here to there might require you to go alone. Do not be afraid of what is awakening in you.

You cannot stay in the same place mentally and spiritually and expect to get from your here to your there. You cannot shake your haters with the same mentality they have. It is time to elevate your mind. Change your thinking, increase your faith.

You stay here I'm going over there.
The blessing is in my over there.

You are close but from HERE you gotta push
AND pray to get THERE.
You cannot stay where you are.

There's nothing wrong with where you are, right?

If it is working for you why try to make it better? That is the pitfall many of us fall in. It is called complacency.

Complacency lies to us telling us I'm ok here. Why rock the boat? Why change it? It's working ok. Comfort is the companion to complacency that makes us feel at ease where we are so we lose the desire to get out the boat. Comfort and complacency are two companions that will make you miss your destination. We undermine our future when we settle for less because we are afraid to think outside the box or even move the box.

You can do better, have better but you cannot stay where you are you gotta go over there to get it. Your over there will come with uncertainty and may appear cloudy but don't worry, trust God to guide you to your destination.

Remember the lepers? They could have stayed at the gate and died but they made a choice to leave the gate. It is time to make a choice. Will you stay where you are or make a choice to let God lead you to better?

God is trying to lead you and where you are going you will have to pray your way through to get there. You are going to have to push your way past what is holding you back. You are going to have to praise your way through to get there. The journey from here to there will be full of obstacles designed to deter you from your destination. Keep pushing, keep praying and keep praising. Whatever you do don't let yourself become stagnant and do not give up because you are so close to your breakthrough.

Whatever you do, don't be fooled into staying where you are. Death is here and life is there. Which will you choose?

**You stay here I'm going over there.
I'm not dying here…………..**

EPILOGUE

My Story

Every word written in this book is about me. There was a time I was dying emotionally and spiritually but something inside me was screaming to live. At the age of 15 I became pregnant and later married the father of my child at 18. I married because it was the right thing to do but that was the wrong reason to marry. As a result I suffered years of physical, verbal and emotional abuse. The emotional and physical wounds I talked about in the book they were my wounds. Some were visible and some were not but each one hurt me deeply in places I kept hidden.

The masks, yeah that was me too. I tried to hide in plain sight and conceal everything that was going on with me. I lost myself trying to be everything to everybody. I lost my identity trying to fit in until one day I decided that would be my last day here. I could no longer take the pain and I just wanted it all to end. But God had other plans....

I can't tell you I had an "Aha" moment and decided to change my course instantly....no it was a process (just like the butterfly). I turned it all over to God. I walked away (or God removed) everything and everyone that was designed to tear me down or destroy me. Only the things (and people) that remained in my life were placed there to build me up. I was under construction and did not even realize it. God could have easily just renovated my life but He knew that the remnants of my past would be a source of distraction. Therefore He called for a total rebuild. He left no room for me to say that I changed my life or anyone else. I know without a shadow of a doubt that had it not been for God I could not be the person I am today. My metamorphous was all part of His plan.

God showed me the real me and I removed my masks. No longer did I have to hide behind false pretenses or to be defined by what others thought of me. My only desire then (and now) is to please God.

I was thirsty, dying for a drink. And out of my desperation I ended up in negative situations with the wrong people but God still was protecting me. Everything that should have been bad for me God used it to strengthen me. From the ashes of my life I arose stronger and wiser with a zeal and fire for God that I would let no one try to extinguish.

It was time to live....truly live. Live the life that God had for me not the one that the world said I should not have.

ABOUT THE AUTHOR

Born and raised in Texas, Albirtha is a very family oriented person. She is a devoted wife and mother and loves her family deeply. She loves to laugh and have fun and often jokingly refers to herself as a person of many layers and personalities. She laughs even in the darkest moments of her life; she says it keeps her from crying. But most of the time you will see her deep in thought.

Albirtha served in the United States Army before attending college and obtaining her Bachelor's degree in nursing. She loves being a nurse as much as she loves serving, preaching, and teaching. As an ordained minister she serves tirelessly in several ministries at her church.

In her spare time she loves to read. One summer, as a child, she earned the Library Achievement Award for reading over 100 books over summer break. She also loves to write and has written several skits and plays.

Albirtha has endured and overcome many hardships. As part of the healing process of her past failures and toxic relationships, Albirtha writes this book to inspire others like her that as bleak as it may seem now there is hope on the horizon. Brought up in the church she always found the church (and God) to be her anchor. Therefore she felt it equally befitting to throw others the same life line that saved her.